TRIVIA-ON-BOOKS

PRESENTS

Rick Riordan's
Percy Jackson's Greek Gods

A TRIVIA GUIDES COLLECTION

Join the trivia club

Foreword

Many read the book, but many don't like it.

Many like the book, but many are not avid fans.

Many call themselves avid fans, but few truly are.

Come test your knowledge with a trivia quiz to the book and see if you have what it takes to be called an avid fan. This is the missing link to separate yourself from the crowd and find out if you really are an avid fan or not.

What will you score?

Editors at

Trivia-On-Books

Table of Contents

TRIVIA-ON-BOOKS

PRESENTS

Rick Riordan's
Percy Jackson's Greek Gods

The First Challenge

Have you read the book?

Question #1

With whom did Athena have a contest?

    a. Arachne

    b. Europa

    c. Selene

    d. Poseidon

ANSWER a

Arachne

Arachne came from a poor family and was left an orphan at a young age. She taught herself to weave and soon became adept at it. She could weave in beautiful sceneries and patterns and became famous for it. She was proud of the fact and refused to pay obeisance to Athena, the goddess of weaving and crafts. Even when Athena appeared in front of Arachne, she only challenged her to a weaving contest. They both began to weave, and Athena was forced to admit that Arachne was very good at her skill. However, when Arachne would not stop blowing her trumpet, Athena hit her on the head with the shuttle of her loom. This humiliated Arachne, who then committed suicide. Taking pity on her,

Athena brought her back to life and made her into a spider, and claimed she would weave forever.

Who was the first creature to be created in Greek mythology?

    a. Ouranus

    b. Kronos

    c. Zeus

    d. Gaea

ANSWER d

Gaea

At first, there was Chaos, but it was not really a creature by itself. From the Chaos, the earth was created, which took on the personality of a living person. The name of this entity was Gaea, the Earth Mother. She is considered to be the first 'person' in existence by the Greeks, and the mother of everyone and everything. She was the first goddess, and it is from her that all the other gods, including the Olympeans, descended.

Question #3

By whom was Ouranus killed?

    a. Gaea

    b. Kronos

    c. Phoebe

    d. Oceanus

ANSWER b

Kronos

Gaea was the first goddess, and she created Ouranus, the sky. The two mated and had twelve children, who were known as the Titans. But she also gave birth to Cyclopes and Hekatonkheires, both of them an ugly species. Ouranus disowned them and threw them into Tartarus, a fiery pit deep in the earth. Gaea hated this and wanted revenge. When Ouranus claimed more power, Gaea gathered her Titan children and proposed they kill Ouranus and free their siblings. Only Kronos agreed to the job, though he was helped by Koios, Iapetus, Krios, and Hyperion. Gaea made Kronos a scythe, and he butchered Ouranus, casting the remains into the sea.

Question #4

Who invented humans?

    a. Zeus

    b. Gaea

    c. Prometheus

    d. Athena

ANSWER c

Prometheus

Prometheus was the son of Iapetus and Klymene. The legend goes that he was clever with his hands. When he was playing at the riverbank, he made a couple of clay figures that looked similar to the Titans, but much smaller in size. The split blood of Ouranus either got into the soil or Prometheus was able to give life to the figures, but they came to life and became the first two humans. Prometheus always retained affection for his creation, and later went to great lengths to give them fire, thus incurring the wrath of Zeus. He also warned the humans about the flood Zeus had planned.

Question #5

Who deposed Kronos as the king of the cosmos?

    a. Zeus

    b. Gaea

    c. Hera

    d. Oceanus

ANSWER a

Zeus

After murdering his father, Kronos became the king of the universe. But his father had cursed him that he too would be deposed in a similar way. This curse prevented him from marrying for a long time, but he finally decided to settle down with his sister, Rhea. When Rhea gave birth to their first child, Hestia, Kronos realized she was very powerful, and swallowed her. Kronos did the same with the next four children that followed, but by then Rhea had had enough. She tricked Kronos and spirited her sixth child away to be raised in safety. When Zeus grew up, he returned to Olympus pretending to be a cupbearer and released his siblings from inside him. Together, they later deposed Kronos.

Question #6

Who was the lord of the underworld?

    a. Tartarus

    b. Hades

    c. Dionysus

    d. Hephaestus

ANSWER b

Hades

When Zeus and his siblings took over from Kronos, the male gods left out the female gods and decided amongst themselves which male god would have dominion over which part of the world. Hades got the Underworld. Before Hades took charge, the Underworld was a mess with souls wandering around to the wrong places. People were judged before they died by other people who could be bribed, and often were. Charon also charged exorbitant amounts to ferry souls across the Styx river. Hades made changes and appointed three souls from the Underworld to make the judgment after people died. He also made sure that each soul was sent to the right place that they deserved: The Fields of Punishment, the Fields of Asphodel, or the Elysium.

Over which city did Athena and Poseidon fight?

    a. Sparta

    b. Olympia

    c. Attica

    d. Amphipolis

ANSWER c

Attica

Attica was one of the biggest and most important cities on the Greek mainland. Poseidon wanted to be its patron god and sought out the citizens with his offer. However, Athena had also decided to do the same, leaving the king's council in confusion. Athena proposed a peaceful contest between them and let the townspeople make the decision based on who could give them the most useful thing. Poseidon created horses and gifted them to the Atticans. Athena gave them the olive tree and told them that it could make them rich and famous. The townspeople chose Athena, making Poseidon angry. He sent a flood to the city and was only appeased when the Atticans, now the Athenians, built a temple for both Athena and Poseidon.

Question #8

Which god was conceived solely by Hera?

a. Prometheus

b. Ares

c. Hephaestus

d. Apollo

Hephaestus

Hera had an argument with Zeus about all the children he was fathering and went off to mother a child all by herself. She managed to do this, but when the baby was born, it was ugly with weak legs. Hera was horrified and threw him down the top of the mountain. Hephaestus was rescued by a Nereid called Thetis, who raised him. When he grew up, Hephaestus decided to go back to Olympus with plenty of gifts for the gods. Everyone was happy with their presents and welcomed him, except for Hera, who was suspicious. But she gradually gave in and sat down in the throne Hephaestus had presented her. It proved to be a mistake, and Hera was immediately bound over tightly by invisible ropes. It was only when Dionysus convinced him to forgive Hera that Hephaestus relented and freed her.

Question #9

Who is the god of warfare?

a. Athena

b. Poseidon

c. Hera

d. Ares

ANSWER d

Ares

Ares was the son of Hera and Zeus. When he was a baby, he broke his father's finger. Ares was looked after by his nanny, Thero, who brought him up in Thrace. Ares grew up learning how to fight, and when he grew up, he returned to Olympia to take his rightful place. He became the god of warfare. He also was the god of strength and courage. The Amazon women are believed to be descended from Ares. Though Athena was also a goddess of warfare, the difference between them was that Athena looked after the strategic aspects of war while Ares was more involved in the bloody and violent aspects.

Which country did Dionysus invade?

a. Syria

b. India

c. China

d. Mesopotamia

ANSWER b

India

Dionysus was the god of wine and the son of Selene and Zeus. When he grew up, he invented wine and claimed a few kingdoms for his own. Where the kings or the people did not submit to him or join his religion, he punished them by inflicting them with madness. Finally, he decided to invade India and set out along with his followers. They took in a lot of towns along the way, but when they reached India, Dionysus was unable to breach the defenses. He and his followers managed to reach the Ganges River, but after one last unsuccessful attack at the fort there, they returned to Greece.

The Second Challenge

Do you know the author?

Question #1

What is *Percy Jackson's Greek Gods* called in the non-US countries?

     a. Percy Jackson's Greek Gods

     b. The Greek Gods Collection

     c. Percy Jackson and the Greek Gods

     d. Percy Jackson – Part 6

ANSWER c

Percy Jackson and the Greek Gods

Percy Jackson's Greek Gods is the original name of the book, first published in the US in August 2014 by Puffin Books, an imprint of Penguin Group. It is an accompaniment book to the series *Percy Jackson and the Olympians*, and could be considered the sixth book of the series. Publishers generally believe that some titles do better in the US and others do better in the rest of the world, because Americans are different. Hence, the title for the UK and the rest of the world was slightly changed to *Percy Jackson and the Greek Gods*.

Question #2

Who did the illustrations for *Percy Jackson and the Greek Gods*?

    a. Rick Riordan

    b. Gary Gianni

    c. John Rocco

    d. Rowena Morrill

ANSWER c

John Rocco

Percy Jackson's Greek Gods has 60 full-color paintings and illustrations depicting the various stories, themes, and plots of the book. These illustrations were done by John Rocco, a celebrated illustrator of children's books. Apart from this book, Rocco is known for creating picture books. Riordan gave the draft to Rocco after he finished each chapter, and left Rocco with a free hand to do the designing. Rocco has also created the Percy Jackson-based theme T-shirts and other items.

Question #3

Who is the narrator of *Percy Jackson's Greek Gods*?

a. Rick Riordan

b. Zeus

c. Thalia Grace

d. Percy Jackson

ANSWER d

Percy Jackson

Percy Jackson is the protagonist of a series of books in which he goes on several adventures. He is the son of Poseidon, the sea god, and hence a demigod. So the narrative is done by Percy Jackson, and while the author chose to stick to most of the original mythology stories, Percy's biases come through in the book. Being Poseidon's son, he believes that Poseidon is the best Greek god, and he tries to give him a positive outlook. According to the author, the book would not have worked as well if narrated by someone else.

Question #4

When was *Percy Jackson's Greek Gods* published?

        a. 2000

        b. 2010

        c. 2014

        d. 2016

ANSWER c

2014

The Percy Jackson series commenced in 2005, the year in which Riordan published his first book, *The Lightning Thief*. After this, the other books in the five-book series appeared at regular intervals every year with the last of them being published in 2009. In 2013, Riordan announced that he would be writing an accompaniment book to the series based on the Greek myths as narrated by Percy Jackson.

Question #5

How did Riordan get inspired to create the character of Percy Jackson?

a. Reading a retelling of old mythologies

b. Bedtime stories he told his son

c. His students gave him the idea

d. He had a dream about the Greek gods

ANSWER b

Bedtime stories he told his son

Riordan's son loved Greek mythology as much as he did. Haley always asked his father to tell him mythologies for bedtime but when Riordan ran out of stories, Haley asked him to come up with more. So Riordan, remembering an assignment he would give his students in which they had to create a demigod and a quest for him or her, created the character of Percy Jackson and gave him a quest. This story became *The Lightning Thief*, the first book in a series of five books. *Percy Jackson's Greek Gods* is an accompaniment book to this series.

Question #6

Who helped Riordan refine his first Percy Jackson book?

    a. His son

    b. His students

    c. His editor

    d. A close friend

ANSWER b

His students

Once his first book was completed, Riordan decided to show it to his students since that age group was his target market anyway. He chose a few students from the sixth, seventh, and eighth grades and asked for their opinion. The children really liked the books, but they also offered plenty of suggestions to Riordan, many of which he incorporated. This helped Riordan refine the character and the books in the series. He claims he was happy he had shown his work to his students as critics.

Question #7

How did Riordan choose which version of the Greek myths to include in the book?

    a. He chose the funniest versions

    b. He chose the versions randomly

    c. He chose the ones that fit best into the overall story

    d. He picked the version he came across first in his research

ANSWER c

He chose the ones that fit best into the overall story

There are many different versions in the legends of Greek mythology depending on when it became popular. Some of these differences are not too distinct while others are significant. Riordan claims that he read up on all the versions and chose the ones that fit best into the overall plot of the story he wanted to tell. He tried to keep his version of the events as close to the original as possible and only modernized the language and gave it a humorous touch.

Question #8

What was the biggest challenge in writing *Percy Jackson's Greek Gods*?

    a. Choosing which version of the myths to include

    b. How to depict some of the gorier details of the myths

    c. Doing the research

    d. Making the book comprehensive as well as interesting

Answer d

Making the book comprehensive as well as interesting

When Riordan decided to write a book for children retelling the Greek mythologies, he had to face certain challenges. One of the biggest problems he had was to make sure that he was able to write the old myths in their entirety, which meant de-emphasizing certain aspects of the stories. He also wanted to include some of the lesser known myths. On the other hand, he had to make sure that these stories were told in a way that would be interesting and fun for children to read. Trying to handle these two objectives together was Riordan's biggest challenge.

Question #9

From where did Riordan do his research for *Percy Jackson's Greek Gods?*

    a. The d'Aulaires retelling

    b. The original myths

    c. The Edith Hamilton retelling

    d. The Kate Benheimer retelling

ANSWER b

The original myths

Since Riordan had been obsessed with Greek mythology since he was in sixth grade, he had read a lot of things and already knew most of the stories. He avoided retellings of the stories and turned to the basic and original myths to create a spin of his own. He used certain reference books as well as websites for his research. One of the websites he recommends is the Theoi Greek Mythology, which gives a brief description of all the gods and their lives. Even though he already was well versed in this subject, he claims he learns something new every time he does any research.

What award did Riordan win for this series of books?

      a. Milner Award

      b. Edgar Award

      c. Mark Twain Award

      d. Rebecca Caudill Award

ANSWER a

Milner Award

Percy Jackson's Greek Gods is the accompaniment volume for *Percy Jackson and the Olympians* series. The series won the Milner Award in 2011 before this book was released. The individual books in the series also were both nominated for and won several awards. The Milner Award seeks to promote reading among schoolchildren in the state of Atlanta USA. The choosing process allows the children to vote for their favorite books and authors, and the winner is the one who gets the most votes.

The Third Challenge

Are you an Avid Fan?

Question #1

What was Riordan's profession before he took up writing full time?

a. Teacher

b. Journalist

c. Football coach

d. Accountant

ANSWER a

Teacher

Riordan came from a family of teachers. Not only were both his parents teachers, but his grandparents were also teachers. As a child, he would think that he could explain a concept better while his teacher was trying to teach. This led him to opt for a teaching career. He opted to teach middle-school children because those are the formative years in a child's life. He had a good rapport with his students, and was sad he had to quit when his writing commitments got too much for him to do justice to his teaching.

What was the first book Riordan wrote?

a. Big Red Tequila

b. Percy Jackson's Greek Gods

c. The Lightning Thief

d. The Maze of Bones

ANSWER a

Big Red Tequila

Riordan has been writing short stories since the 1970s. Though he continued to write, he never got published. His first book that got published was Big Red Tequila, a crime story about a Texan detective who returns home to solve the case of his father's murder. Jackson Tres Navarre also gets in trouble with the Mafia and gets embroiled in the local politics. This book was published in June 1997. Riordan wrote a number of other novels in the series with Tres Navarre as the protagonist and detective.

Question #3

What was Riordan's passion before he took up writing?

    a. Theatre

    b. Drawing cartoons

    c. History

    d. Music

ANSWER d

Music

As a young kid in school, Riordan wanted to be a writer. But somehow, this dream got shafted aside when he went to college. There, he got into the music scene big time and wanted to have his own rock band. He even grew a mustache, beard, and long hair to go with the image of a rock star. His college job was playing music at different events during the weekends. He learned the guitar and became adept at both playing guitar and songwriting.

Question #4

What is the name of Riordan's blog?

    a. A History of Mythology

      b. Myth and Mystery

    c. Musings of a Greek God

      d. Blogging with Gods

ANSWER b

Myth and Mystery

Riordan started writing his blog in 2005, around the time his first book, *The Lightning Thief,* was published. He named the blog *Myths and Mystery* for obvious reasons – he wanted to explore the myths and mysteries behind the themes of Greek mythology he was using in his books. Riordan shares snippets of his personal life in his blog, as well as all the information about his books. He also talks about books, the publishing industry and other things that interest him and his fans in the blog.

Question #5

What was Riordan's first novel driven by?

    a. A need to prove himself

    b. Love

    c. A desire for fame

    d. Homesickness

Answer d

Homesickness

When Riordan asked his teachers and other writers what he should write about, he always got the clichéd answer that he should write about what he knows. This puzzled and frustrated him at first. But when he moved away from Texas to San Francisco, he began to think of his old life back in Texas and missed it terribly. He wrote a book set in Texas, and it got published. This was when he realized that he did write about what he knew, but he had to distance himself from it before he could write about it.

Question #6

Who helped Riordan hone his writing skills as a child?

    a. His father

    b. His aunt

    c. His teacher

    d. Writing workshops

ANSWER c

His teacher

Riordan attributes a lot of his success to his teachers. He especially remembers Ms. Pabst, his English teacher in the eighth grade. She read his stories and encouraged him by telling him that he should get published. She even tried to get him to send his stories to a magazine. She introduced him to mythology as well, and this was when he developed his love for reading as he began to read books about Norse and Greek mythologies. He also was introduced to *The Lord of the Rings*, which he loved. Riordan advises all aspiring writers to find a good mentor like his old teacher.

Question #7

What affected Riordan about living in Texas?

    a. The gun culture

  b. The storytelling tradition

    c. The local food

    d. Religion

ANSWER b

The storytelling tradition

Riordan grew up in San Antonio, Texas. He remembers an idyllic childhood. Both his parents were teachers. Riordan was not too interested in sports and enjoyed playing games with friends instead. He also loved music and learned to play the guitar. But most of all, Riordan enjoyed the camping trips during which everyone would sit around the campfire and tell stories. This storytelling tradition in Texas influenced Riordan deeply, and he claims this is what got him interested in telling stories. He relates this to his love of mythology as well.

Question #8

What is Riordan's goal in writing books for children?

    a. He wants to make money

    b. He wants to get the satisfaction of seeing his name in print

    c. He loves writing for the sake of writing

    d. He wants the reluctant readers to discover the joys of reading

ANSWER d

He wants the reluctant readers to discover the joys of reading

Riordan himself was a reluctant reader when he was a child. It was only when he read books like *The Lord of the Rings* that he began to enjoy reading. However, he was a slow reader and was not a great student either. When Riordan was a teacher, he tried to get even the low-performing children to read. He had the same experience with his own children, who were reluctant readers and he had a hard time finding books they could enjoy. With this idea in mind, Riordan writes his books for children in the hope that even the backbenchers would pick up a book inspired by his stories.

Question #9

How does Riordan like to write?

    a. He writes on the fly

   b. He plans each chapter in advance

  c. He outlines the plot before writing

   d. He does his research hands on

ANSWER b

He plans each chapter in advance

Riordan likes to plan his stories out in advance. He roughly outlines each chapter before he begins to write. This helps him to know and plan what to write. Even if he thinks it's not so good, he still jots it down and works his way from what he calls the first draft. Riordan claims that because of this technique, he rarely experiences writer's block because he already knows what he is going to write by the time he actually gets down to it. He sometimes gets stuck on smaller things, but they quickly get resolved.

Question #10

How many pages does Riordan write in a day?

a. Five

b. Ten

c. He finishes a chapter a week

d. He has no fixed schedule

ANSWER d

He has no fixed schedule

Like many writers, Riordan has his own writing process—something that works for him. But unlike many who plan their days, he has no fixed schedule. His speed usually depends on what he is doing. His first draft tends to go fast, and he works for about five hours a day. But when he is revising after the initial draft, it takes more time and on a highly productive day, he can complete up to five pages. He also advises budding writers to write at least a page a day to keep up the enthusiasm.

The Moment of Truth

Results May Vary

Based on the difficulty of the questions you are an Avid Fan if you've received less than "2" wrong.

<u>Review This Book!</u>

Made in the USA
Middletown, DE
01 February 2020